पेंसिल

FSC® 100% FSC-C095304
MICADOR
ESSENTIAL PENCIL 6B
ESSENTIAL PENCIL 4B
ESSENTIAL PENCIL 2B
ESSENTIAL PENCIL HB

Pencil

रबर

Eraser

पेंसिल शार्पनर

Pencil Sharpner

रंगीन पेंसिल

Coloured Pencil

रंगीन चॉक

Coloured Chauk

दफ्ती

Clipboard

कॉपी

Copy

पानी के रंग

Water Colours

पोस्टर रंग

Poster Colours

स्केच पैन

Sketch Pen

Brush

स्टेपलर

Steplar

कैंची

Scissor

ग्लू

FABER-CASTELL
White Glue 100ml
For Art and Craft
Easy Squeeze

Glue

टेप स्टैंड

Tape Stand

ज्यामिति बॉक्स

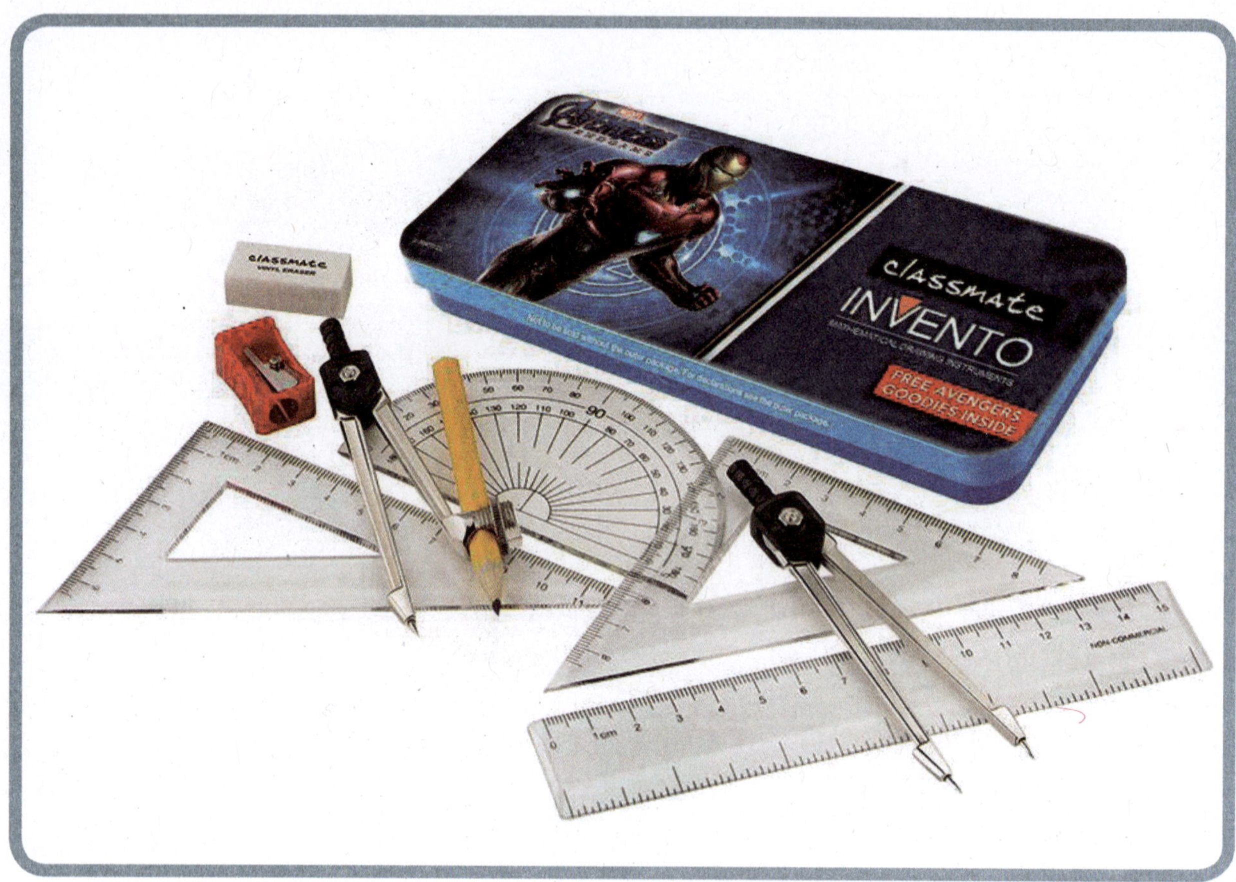

Geometry Box